Maximize Your Earnings with a Health Savings Account

Also Available by Keith Dorney

Becoming Financially Independent book series

Best Debt Elimination Plan: *Debt Management Strategies that Get You Out of Debt Quickly and Economically*

A Beginners Guide to Roth IRAs and 401(k)-Type Plans: *Contribution, Conversion, and Withdrawal Strategies for Building Tax-Free Wealth*

DIY Stock and Securities Investing: *Investment Strategies for Building Wealth and Attaining Financial Independence*

Maximize Your Earnings with a Health Savings Account: *Learn how a Health Savings Account can save you money. Take advantage of 4 tax breaks and seriously consider investing some of those contributions.*

Maximize Your Earnings with a Health Savings Account

Keith Dorney CFP® MA

https://keithdorney.com

Copyright © 2026
by Keith Dorney Books
All Rights Reserved

ISBN: 979-8-9887374-4-5

Disclaimer:

The information contained within this book is not and should not be construed as financial or investment advice: Advice can only be given once an advisor has a deeper understanding of an individual's complete financial situation. The information in this book should be considered of a general educational nature, not financial or investment advice.

This book will educate you with what is hoped to be correct and up-to-date information, but no warranty or promise is made that everything is 100% accurate.

This book is published as a print-on-demand book for a reason: I update it every year. I take pride in providing only the most up-to-date information in easy-to-understand language.

To Katherine—my best friend, wife, tireless editor, and love of my life

Table of Contents

Detailed Table of Contents 73

A Diamond Among Your Employee Benefits 9

Choosing the Right Insurance Coverage 21

Choosing the Right Health Savings Account 31

The Importance of Medical Record Keeping 37

HSA Eligible Medical Expenses 43

HSA Ineligible Medical Expenses 47

Health Savings Account Contribution Limits 49

Developing a Withdrawal Strategy 51

HSA Withdrawals in Retirement 58

State Income Taxes and Your Withdrawals 61

Be Smarter with Your Money 63

About Keith Dorney 71

A Diamond Among Your Employee Benefits

A Health Savings Account can save you money. I'm not talking about just a few bucks here — I'm talking about substantial savings, more than any other tax-advantaged account.

If your employer doesn't offer a Health Savings Account (HSA), along with a high-deductible health plan option, they are in the minority. But don't fret—chances are they'll add one soon. Most private health insurance plans and healthcare exchanges offer plenty of HSA options.

More employers have added this option not only in response to rising healthcare costs and the passage of the Patient Protection and Affordable Care Act, but also in anticipation of the next rendition of our national healthcare system.

One thing is certain: Health Savings Accounts (HSAs) are here to stay. It's one of the few things beloved by both political parties. If anything, they are becoming an even more integral part of the solution to the problem of escalating healthcare costs.

Back in the early 2000s, after taking a deep dive into what was then a brand-new tax-advantaged account, I couldn't believe all the tax advantages an HSA afforded. I knew this translated into more money saved and earned, but I had no idea how much until I opened my own HSA.

It's tough keeping up with inflation, the cost of living, and runaway healthcare costs: It seems to get harder every year. Adding a Health Savings Account can help.

Did you know you can invest your HSA funds? It's true. Just like other tax-advantaged accounts, including 401(k)s and IRAs, you can invest in ETFs, mutual funds, and individual stocks and bonds. The difference is the *four* tax advantages you get with an HSA, including tax-free earnings.

I recommend using one of the following three HSA strategies, depending on your risk tolerance and individual situation. These strategies are discussed further in the *Developing a Withdrawal Strategy* chapter.

1. **Take the Money Now** – Estimate your out-of-pocket medical expenses for the coming year and deposit that amount, including any employer contributions, into your HSA. Tax-free funds can then be withdrawn as needed to pay for your

qualified medical expenses throughout the plan year. Unused funds stay in your account for use in subsequent years.

2. **The HSA Double-Dip** – It's just like number one, but you try to deposit the yearly maximum contribution allowed every year into your HSA, even if it's more than your projected medical costs. Invest the excess for your financial future.

3. **Take It to the Max** – Like number two, deposit the maximum yearly amount allowed by law into your HSA. Do not reimburse yourself for any medical expenses. Save those medical receipts for future reimbursement in the years to come. Pay for your out-of-pocket medical expenses with non-HSA money and invest those contributions for your financial future instead. Enjoy a higher after-tax rate of return on your investments because of all those tax advantages.

Given four tax breaks, your HSA may very well be your top-performing account. If you can afford it, seriously consider using your HSA exclusively as a wealth-building tool by employing this "take it to the max" strategy.

Get Ready for Open Enrollment

Check your benefits page now so you'll be ready for open enrollment. Open enrollment is usually the only time of the year you can change your health plan. Depending on the source, you may have many choices or only one. Look for the health plans that come with a Health Savings Account.

Flexible Spending Account versus HSA

A Health Savings Account is like a Flexible Spending Account, which is another employer-sponsored account you may not be offered. Like a Health Savings Account, tax-free dollars can be deposited and used to pay your medical expenses. Although HSAs and Flexible Spending Accounts share this characteristic, that's where the similarities end.

An HSA is an individual account, not an employer-controlled one like a Flexible Spending Account. Even if your employer is nice enough to kick a few bucks into your HSA as part of your benefit (many do), it's still your account and your money, and you have several options as to what to do with it.

Additionally, unlike Flexible Spending Accounts, there is no "use it or lose it" rule with HSAs. That means unused money remains in your account for future use. Use it to pay for your medical expenses for next year, ten years from now, or in retirement.

Qualified Medical Expenses
Only qualified medical expenses can be withdrawn tax-free from your HSA and include:

- Next year's medical expenses
- Spouse's medical expenses in ten years
- Dependent's current medical expenses
- Certain medical procedures and services that are not covered by your insurance

Want a Quadruple Tax Break?

An HSA is the undisputed winner when it comes to tax-advantaged accounts. No other account on the planet offers as many tax breaks.

If you can, take advantage of all four tax breaks this year and in future years. Why not take advantage of every tax break your Uncle Sam affords?

Tax Break #1
Your first tax break comes with your yearly contribution. You can contribute to an HSA every year you have an HSA-eligible high-deductible health plan. For family plans, that's up to $8,750 in 2026. The maximum for individual plans is $4,400.

That's the total contributions both you and your employer can make for the plan year.

Your contribution is subtracted from your gross income for the year. This saves you taxes in the year of the contribution and reduces your AGI (adjusted gross income), which could make you eligible for other tax advantages.

For example, making an HSA contribution may qualify you to make a Roth IRA contribution. Or maybe that lower AGI now makes you eligible for other benefits, like deducting some of your student loan interest or part of your medical premium.

Making traditional 401(k)-type plan contributions, traditional IRA contributions, and contributing to an HSA are all ways you can reduce your tax bill this year and in subsequent years. The higher your marginal tax bracket, the more you save.

Tax Break #2
As mentioned in Tax Break #1, HSA contributions act like traditional contributions and reduce your tax burden for the contribution year. Your HSA contribution takes it a step further. Assuming qualified withdrawals, you *never* pay tax on that contribution.

With a traditional 401(k)-type plan or traditional IRA contributions, you must pay tax on that contribution—at ordinary income tax rates no less—upon withdrawal.

Tax Break #3

Think of a Health Savings Account as an IRA or 401(k)-type plan on steroids. It combines the tax-saving and income-generating characteristics of both traditional and Roth accounts.

As mentioned, with a pre-tax or traditional contribution, you get a tax deduction, but you've got to pay tax on both the contribution and earnings upon withdrawal. With a Roth contribution, you get tax-free earnings but no tax deduction.

With a Health Savings Account, you get the advantages of both: *A tax deduction plus tax-free earnings* upon qualified withdrawal! You get the tax advantages of *both* traditional and Roth contributions.

Most HSA custodians allow you to invest unused funds for the future. Any interest, dividends, or capital gains are completely tax-free per qualified withdrawal.

Tax Break #4

Your final tax break is realized only if you make your contribution via payroll deduction through your employer. Your employer will *not* deduct payroll taxes from your contribution, saving you another 6.2% (Social Security) and 1.45% (Medicare) on your contribution.

Realize that payroll taxes *are* deducted from your 401(k)-type plan contributions. Same if you're making your own IRA contributions: Payroll taxes have already been deducted from that money.

That's why, if you have a choice, you want to make your HSA contributions via payroll deductions. If you purchase private insurance, you won't benefit from this last tax break, but you still enjoy the first three.

Unused Money Rolls Forward

It makes sense to invest any unused money in your Health Savings Account. This takes advantage of Tax Breaks #2 and #3 (tax-free principal and earnings).

Investing that unused money allows you to grow your HSA for later. And because of those tax breaks, you'll enjoy an after-tax return greater than in any other account (investment returns being equal).

Those unused contributions and any earnings (interest, dividends, and capital gains) can be utilized tax-free not only for your own future out-of-pocket medical expenses but for your spouse and other dependent expenses too, *regardless of whether they are covered under your health insurance.*

If you sign up for long-term care insurance, those premium payments are an HSA-eligible expense too. However, there are IRS-imposed limits as to how much of your premium is HSA-eligible, depending on your age.

For these reasons and more, try to max out your HSA contributions each year you are eligible if you can. Even though you can only contribute to your HSA in the years you are covered by a high-deductible health plan, you can use that money to pay for your out-of-pocket medical expenses anytime, *even in years when you are covered by non-HSA eligible health insurance.*

When You Reach Age 65

Once you reach age 65, your options for tax-free withdrawals increase even more. Money can be withdrawn tax-free and used to pay:

- Medicare premiums (A, B & D)
- Spouse's Medicare premiums (A, B & D)
- Long-term care expenses

- Long-term care insurance premiums
- Your medical expenses

I wouldn't worry about accumulating too much cash. According to a Fidelity® study, on average, a couple reaching age 65 in 2026 will need north of $300,000 during retirement for medical expenses not covered by Medicare.

That's *average*, so some of us will need more, some less. Plus, medical costs could grow at a rate even greater than inflation.

Substitute for Long Term Care Insurance

Then there's the potential need for long-term care. Nothing can ravage an estate faster than the need for long-term care. According to a Genworth® study, private room nursing home care runs six figures a year in many states.

An HSA can act as an alternative to the sky-high cost of long-term care insurance. Think of it as insuring yourself. Remember, those thousands of dollars of premium payments are not refunded by the insurance company if you don't need long-term care, and the odds are you won't.

Best Case Scenario

So, what happens if you are successful with your investment plan and rack up a substantial amount of earnings, and you, your spouse, and your dependents all end up being extremely healthy and not in need of long-term care? We can all wish...

If this best-case scenario unfolds, what happens to the money taken out when there is no credit for healthcare expenses? It depends on your age.

If you're age 65 or older, there is no penalty, but you must pay tax on your withdrawals. So now your HSA becomes the equivalent of a really good investment vehicle like a traditional (pre-tax) IRA or 401(k)-type plan instead of a supercharged one.

If you're under 65 and choose to tap non-credited funds, all your advantages are lost. Not only do you have to pay tax, but a 20% penalty is also assessed. Try to avoid this option if possible.

Not For Everyone

Health Savings Accounts aren't for everyone. A high-deductible health plan, which you must have to make an HSA contribution, means your share of the medical insurance premium will be lower than other plans, but your out-of-pocket costs will be higher if you need care.

I've seen employer-sponsored plans where the overall difference in costs between their low and high-deductible health plans is minimal, making the high-deductible plan and HSA a more desirable choice.

Other employers offer plans with larger margins between the costs of their health plans. That's why, during every open enrollment, it's important to check all your healthcare options.

I know a lot about HSAs, health insurance plans, and investing. I regularly counsel employees about their employee benefits, and I'm a CFP®. Now that I'm retired and making withdrawals from my own HSA, I'm thankful I followed these same strategies.

Choosing the Right Insurance Coverage

To realize all the benefits of a Health Savings Account, you must be enrolled in what is known as a high-deductible health plan (HDHP). That's the only way you're eligible to make an HSA contribution for that plan year.

Consider yourself lucky if you've got employer-sponsored health insurance. Chances are you're already offered plenty of choices, including HDHP health plans that come with HSA privileges. If you're getting health insurance privately or otherwise, securing good, affordable health insurance can be more challenging.

Wellness Services

Regardless of how you procure your health insurance, wellness services will be offered. Historically, many services are low-cost or free.

One preventive care visit per year is free of charge, regardless of the insurance tier you choose. Other preventive procedures and tests, including screenings, hospice, prenatal and postnatal care, plus eye exams and glasses for children, may be covered without regard to deductible, co-pay, or co-insurance.

That means many of the services you need will be at no cost or low cost to you, even if you choose one of the high-deductible health plan options.

Other free or low-cost services include:

- Screening for gestational diabetes
- Testing for the human papillomavirus (HPV)
- Sexually transmitted diseases
- Contraceptive methods and counseling
- Breastfeeding support, supplies, and counseling
- Domestic violence issues

Read on before deciding if a high-deductible health plan, along with a Health Savings Account, is the right choice for you.

Low-Deductible Health Plan

If you visit the doctor frequently, take multiple medications, or anticipate high healthcare costs for the year, a lower deductible plan may be preferable. Medical expenses (deductible, copayment, and coinsurance) will be lower than with a high-deductible plan when you need care and may be more economical even though you pay a higher premium.

Some companies are taking an "all-in" approach to Health Savings Accounts and offering one in association with all their tiers of insurance. Other employers have been slower to adapt and may not even offer an HSA-compatible option.

Become familiar with your healthcare offerings before open enrollment. Also, make it a habit every year to tally up your family's medical expenses from the previous year. That information makes it easier to decide which healthcare option will work best for you in the coming year.

High-Deductible Health Plan

If your projected healthcare costs are small to moderate for the coming year, a high-deductible health plan (HDHP), along with the advantages of an HSA, would be a good choice. Remember, you can only make HSA contributions in the years you're covered by an HDHP.

Even though you'll have higher medical costs when you need care, you pay a lower premium than with lower deductible/higher premium plans. Plus, you get all those tax breaks an HSA affords.

Even after the deductible is met, your out-of-pocket costs could be higher because HDHPs have higher copayment/coinsurance costs than the higher premium plans, at least until the out-of-pocket maximum is reached. This is how most insurance plans work.

The advantages of an HSA, of course, must be factored into your healthcare coverage decision. Consider all the tax breaks and the ability to save and invest for future healthcare expenses. The more money you make and the higher your tax bracket, the more you save.

To qualify as an HDHP, a health plan must meet both the minimum deductible and maximum out-of-pocket limits.

Minimum Deductible Limits

HSA-compatible health plans must meet or exceed the IRS-defined deductible limit to qualify as a high-deductible health plan. The following limits are for tax year 2026:

Minimum Deductible Limits	
Self-Only Coverage	$1,700
Family Coverage	$3,400

Out-of-Pocket Maximums

In addition to meeting minimum deductible standards, HSA-compatible health plans must have out-of-pocket maximums that don't exceed the maximums. The following limits are for tax year 2026:

Out-of-Pocket Maximums	
Self-Only Coverage	$8,500
Family Coverage	$17,000

Understanding "Insurance Speak"

To fully understand your choices, you'll need to be able to interpret "health insurance-speak."

Premium

This is the monthly amount you pay to maintain your health insurance. Your employer may pay for all or part of it. Any remainder is paid by you via a payroll deduction, in most cases.

If you have non-employer-sponsored health insurance, you pay the whole premium, unless you qualify for government benefits.

Deductible

The deductible, which does *not* include your part of the monthly premium, is the amount you must pay out-of-pocket for medical care before your health insurance kicks in. Some services, like your yearly wellness visit with your doctor, may have no deductible, copayment, or coinsurance. (That means they're free.)

Other services may have no deductible, but you still have a copayment or coinsurance. ("Having no deductible," often phrased as "not counting toward the deductible," means the same thing.)

Coinsurance

This is the percentage you pay for a covered healthcare service once the deductible is met (or if the service has no deductible). The higher the tier you choose, the more expensive the premium, but the lower the coinsurance and deductible. Rather than a percentage, some plans charge a fixed amount for covered healthcare services, which is known as a **copayment**.

Insurance Tiers

Most likely, you'll be offered several "tiers" of insurance. Most HDHP options that are HSA-eligible will be found in the lower tiers (lowest premiums but highest deductibles, co-insurance, and co-pays); However, more HSA-compatible health plans are appearing in the higher tiers, so be sure to explore all your options.

I've found that many employers are reluctant to use the phrase "high deductible" when describing their plans because of a possible negative connotation. Don't let that fool you. If the health plan comes with an HSA, it meets the requirements that are set forth for high-deductible plans.

Many healthcare providers use colors to differentiate between their plans: The lowest tier is called the bronze option, then silver, gold, and platinum. Your company or private plan may use different lingo.

Understanding Coverage Acronyms

Once you start looking at your actual health insurance options, you'll have to learn some more "insurance-speak," unfortunately. These confusing acronyms have to do with the network of medical professionals available to you.

Most medical insurers have adopted the "contained network" concept to help manage skyrocketing costs. Insurance companies negotiate set prices for healthcare with these providers, and you are afforded lower prices with them. If you seek care out of network, you pay more.

HMO (Health Maintenance Organization)
Usually, the most inclusive of your choices. That means you must use the organization's doctors and services (except in emergencies) provided under the plan. Often, these services are found all under "one roof." You must live in a specific geographic service area where the service center(s) are located. Kaiser Permanente® is the largest and best-known HMO.

EPO (Exclusive Provider Organization)
No, this wasn't a character from Star Wars. An EPO works much like an HMO: The big difference is that those approved medical providers aren't necessarily all in one place. You must use doctors, hospitals, and specialists in the EPO network, except in an emergency.

PPO (Preferred Provider Organization)
PPOs contract with doctors, hospitals, and specialists that form a network of care. Care is more affordable using the network. Going outside the network is allowed and covered, albeit at a higher cost to you.

HDHP (High-Deductible Health Plan)

You must have an HDHP to qualify to make an HSA contribution.

Choosing the Right Health Savings Account

HSA custodians are those who meet federal requirements and are qualified to host accounts. Some offer nothing more than "checking accounts," where you deposit money and then make tax-free withdrawals to reimburse yourself for your out-of-pocket medical expenses for the year.

You want an HSA custodian that *offers investment options* in addition to the services mentioned above. With employer-sponsored health insurance, unfortunately, it's your employer who chooses the custodian, and they might not have chosen one who does.

That's OK. Go down to HR, smile politely, and ask if they'd mind switching to a different Health Savings Account. You might even explain to them *why* you want them to do this: Maybe they haven't yet heard of my "Maximize Your Earnings" strategy?

That's probably not going to work, but there's no need to fret. Your Health Savings Account is yours, not your employer's, and you can have it with whatever custodian you choose. This is true even if your employer makes deposits to your HSA or matches a portion of your contributions (many do).

Simply transfer those employer-supplied funds over to the HSA of your choosing, the one with the great investment options, after each deposit. It's perfectly fine to have more than one HSA. When your employer makes more deposits next year into that now-empty account, transfer those funds over to your new HSA too.

More employers are becoming hip to my "Maximize your Earnings" strategy, and hopefully, the HSA custodial account you are offered has investment options. Unless it's a real dog plan (high fees and poor investment choices), it's easiest to stick with your employer's custodial choice if you can.

Minimize Your Investment Expenses

You've got to be careful—HSA fees and the quality of investment options vary widely from custodian to custodian. Remember, one of the basic tenets of successful investing is to keep your investment expenses low.

Review the administration fee for maintaining your HSA. Are there brokerage, loads, or sales charges to buy and sell investments? How about a yearly fee?

If you choose mutual funds as your investment vehicle of choice, those fees mentioned above are on top of each mutual fund's expense ratio. When you add all those expenses up, sometimes that represents a lot to make up just to break even!

I look for low fees and superior investment opportunities when searching for a custodian. Remember, not all HSA custodians offer accounts with investment options, let alone with low fees and desirable options, so be sure to choose carefully.

Index Funds Versus Actively Managed Funds

Index mutual funds are a great way to keep your expenses super low. A good index mutual fund should charge you no more than one-quarter of one percent per year. Some of the better ones charge much, much less.

Index mutual funds are "passively" managed. By buying and holding the same securities of the fund's target index, investment fees are minimized, and you're pretty much guaranteed to return what the index returns.

Managers of "actively" managed mutual funds attempt to outperform their benchmark index through the active trading of securities. This generates investment fees ten times plus that of a similar-invested index fund. That disparity in investment fees must be made up by the manager year after year after year just to break even with an index fund.

Most actively managed mutual funds don't outperform their benchmark index. That's why, especially over the long term, it's hard to beat a diversified portfolio of index funds.

There are actively managed mutual funds that *justify their higher expense ratio with superior returns* year after year, but they are far and few between. Make sure index mutual funds (or exchange-traded funds) are among your custodian's choices.

Exchange-Traded Funds
An indexed exchange-traded fund (ETF) operates similarly to an index mutual fund but is bought and sold through an exchange via a securities broker. Depending on the fees you're charged to buy and sell ETFs, this is potentially another low-cost option for your investment plan.

Investing with Vanguard®

Even though I am not affiliated with the Vanguard Group® or receive any compensation from them, I freely admit to being a fan.

Are there other companies that offer a good deal for your money? There are: Look for low expense ratios and favorable returns relative to a reliable benchmark. BlackRock® is another favorite.

BlackRock's iShares® ETFs follow their benchmark index with precision and do it at a low cost. BlackRock is also the custodian of one of my favorite 401(k)-type plans, the federal government's Thrift Savings Account or TSP.

Vanguard® and BlackRock® are not custodians for private Health Savings Accounts, but there are lots of custodians of HSAs who offer their products. Hopefully, your health care provider's HSA offers these options.

Recommendations for HSA Custodian

HSA Bank®

This is a good choice if you like to trade individual securities and/or ETFs. They offer a brokerage window through a partnership with TD Ameritrade®, which allows you to trade stocks, bonds, and ETFs. (That includes ETFs with no

brokerage charges from Vanguard®.)
www.hsabank.com

Fidelity®
Fidelity® is a relatively new (fall of 2018) player in the individual HSA marketplace. Take advantage of their low-cost mutual funds, ETFs, and low-cost trading platform. *https://www.fidelity.com*

The Importance of Good Medical Record Keeping

The cornerstone of efficient management of your HSA is good medical record-keeping. It's best to stay on Uncle Sam's good side when you make qualified withdrawals.

Even if you choose a low-deductible health plan and use your employer's Flexible Spending Account instead of an HSA, good record-keeping is also important. Plus, using accurate medical expense records from the previous year is the best way to estimate next year's projected healthcare expenses, which is important because of Flexible Spending Accounts' "use it or lose it" mandate.

If you decide on an HSA and high-deductible health plan, you also need to keep an accurate accounting of those yearly out-of-pocket expenses. If you're ever audited by the IRS, that friendly IRS auditor is going to want to see those reimbursed medical receipts match up with your HSA withdrawals.

Consider scanning all tax-related documents for easier storage, better security, and hassle-free retrieval in the future. The IRS has been accepting scanned documents instead of paper receipts for years as proof of expense.

Maximizing Your Tax-free Earnings

One HSA strategy (*Take it to the Max*) is to pay most or all your medical expenses out-of-pocket rather than reimbursing your HSA and instead invest those contributions. This takes advantage of HSA Tax Break #3 (tax-free earnings).

The idea is to take full advantage of this tax break and generate a bunch of tax-free earnings on those contributions. It's another great way to build your wealth over your working years.

You need to put those unreimbursed medical receipts in a safe place. They act as a "credit" to your HSA, allowing you *at any point in the future* to withdraw that amount *tax-free*.

For instance, tax-free cash can be withdrawn from your HSA for medical expenses that occurred 8 years ago (assuming you had not withdrawn funds from your HSA previously for those same expenses or took a federal tax deduction for those expenses in that tax year).

If your income tax return gets audited, that friendly IRS auditor is going to want to see those receipts from 8 years ago, as well as your tax return from that year too.

Might as well get into the good habit right now of knowing exactly where every penny of your healthcare expenditures goes and then putting that paperwork somewhere you'll be able to find it in the future. Dedicate a file for this purpose or consider digital storage.

IRS Form 8889

IRS Form 8889 (http://www.irs.gov/pub/irs-pdf/f8889.pdf) is where you report both your contributions and withdrawals from your HSA. File it with your tax returns each year you've contributed and/or made a withdrawal. It's also the form beneficiaries use to report their inheritance to the IRS.

The medical expenses that are HSA eligible are the same expenses that the IRS deems eligible for the itemized tax deduction on Schedule 1040, and the same expenses allowed for Flexible Spending Accounts (FSAs) and Health Reimbursement Accounts (HRAs).

The itemized federal tax deduction, however, is only available for medical expenses exceeding 7.5% of your adjusted gross income in 2026. As an example, say your AGI is $100,000 with $8,000 in medical expenses. Only $500 of those expenses are eligible for itemized deductions. The remaining $7,500 is an eligible HSA expense, but not the $500 itemized deduction (no double dipping).

IRS Form 1099-SA

You should receive an IRS Form 1099-SA from your HSA custodian if distributions were made during the plan year. If box three of your form shows distribution code 1, you're good to go. That means your custodian reported all distributions were for qualified medical expenses.

You do not want to see a distribution code 5 on your 1099-SA. That means some of the money distributed was not for qualified medical expenses.

You'll have to pay tax on that amount on top of a 20% penalty. If you're under age 65, avoid making non-qualified distributions from your HSA at all costs; Otherwise, all your tax advantages will be lost.

Once you reach age 65, the 20% penalty is waived, but you still must pay tax on non-qualified distributions at ordinary income tax rates. As mentioned previously, your tax advantages now are the equivalent of making qualified withdrawals from a traditional IRA or pre-tax employer account. It's still a pretty good deal.

Ideally, try to keep that money for future medical expenses and insurance premiums if you can. That way, you'll save the most money.

HSA Eligible Medical Expenses

Keep accurate medical records for your *spouse and dependents* listed on your tax return, as well as for yourself. These expenses act as "credits" too, *regardless of whether they're on your plan.*

This is a partial list. Updated complete lists can be found at: *https://www.irs.gov/pub/irs-pdf/p502.pdf*

- Acupuncture
- Abortion
- Alcoholism
- Ambulance
- Annual Physical Examination
- Artificial Limb
- Artificial Teeth
- Bandages
- Birth Control Pills
- Body Scan
- Braille Books and Magazines
- Breast Pumps and Supplies
- Breast Reconstruction Surgery
- Chiropractor
- Christian Science Practitioner
- Contact Lenses
- Crutches
- Dental Treatment

- Diagnostic Devices
- Disabled Dependent Care Expenses
- Drug Addiction
- Drugs
- Eye Exam
- Eyeglasses
- Eye Surgery
- Fertility Enhancement
- Guide Dog or Other Service Animal
- Hearing Aids
- Home Care
- Hospital Services
- Laboratory Fees
- Lactation Expenses
- Lead-Based Paint Removal
- Lodging
- Long-Term Care
- Long-Term Care Insurance Premiums
- Medicines
- Menstrual Products (Covid 19-related legislation)
- Nursing Home
- Nursing Services
- Operations
- Optometrist
- Organ Donors
- Osteopath
- Oxygen
- Physical Examination
- Pregnancy Test Kit
- Prosthesis
- Psychiatric Care

Psychoanalysis	Transportation
Psychologist	Vasectomy
Special Education	Vision Correction Surgery
Sterilization	
Stop-Smoking Programs	Weight-Loss Program (doctor-prescribed)
Surgery	Wheelchair
Therapy	Wig
Transplants	X-ray

Deductibility of Long-Term Care Insurance Premiums

HSA-qualified withdrawals for long-term care insurance premiums are limited by age. The following are the maximum *yearly* allowances (indexed for inflation) for the tax year 2026:

age ~ maximum yearly allowance

age 40 and under ~ $500

age 41-50 ~ $930

age 51-60 ~ $1,860

age 61-70 ~ $4,960

age 71 and up ~ $6,200

HSA *Ineligible* Medical Expenses

This is a partial list. Find more complete and up-to-date information at: *https://www.irs.gov/pub/irs-pdf/p502.pdf*

Baby Sitting	Illegal Operations and Treatments
Controlled Substances	Insurance Premiums
Cosmetic Surgery	Maternity Clothes
Dancing Lessons	Medicines and Drugs from Other Countries
Diaper Service	Some Nonprescription Drugs and Medicines
Electrolysis/Hair Removal	Nutritional Supplements
Funeral Expenses	Personal Use Items
Future Medical Care	Swimming Lessons
Hair Transplant	Teeth Whitening
Health Club Dues	Veterinary Fees
Household Help	Weight-Loss Programs

Health Savings Account Contribution Limits

Because of the advantages of investing in an HSA, every effort should be made to max it out every year, even at the expense of contributing to other tax-advantaged accounts (matched money from your employer excluded).

HSA Contribution Limits

The following are the maximum contributions allowed for 2026 plans:

HSA Contribution Limits	
Self-Only Coverage	$4,400
Family Coverage	$8,750

HSA "Catch-Up" Contribution

Beginning with the coverage year you turn 55, you are eligible to add an extra $1,000 to your contribution limit. This is true even if your birthday falls on December 31st and is the same amount for self-only and family coverage.

HSA Contributions and Working Spouses

If you're married and each of you chooses a high-deductible health plan with an HSA option, how much can you contribute? You're limited to the family amount ($8,750 for 2026) *combined*. You can each have your own account, but combined, you can't contribute more than the family maximum.

Even though you'll be opening two accounts and possibly be charged more fees, it's best that you each have your own account. You don't want to miss out on any employer contribution or match that might be offered.

Plus, when you reach age 55, with two separate accounts, you can contribute an extra $1,000 a year. (Each spouse can take advantage of the $1,000 "catch-up" amount, but you need two accounts to do so.)

Developing a Withdrawal Strategy

Besides how much to contribute, you also need to decide how much to take out and when. Considering all principal and earnings accrue tax-free upon qualified withdrawal in an HSA, it makes sense to invest at least some of your contributions (or all of them) to take advantage of that attribute.

The idea is to pay some, most, or all your medical expenses out-of-pocket throughout your working years, all the while investing those yearly HSA contributions. If done right, you could have some serious tax-free bank come retirement.

Keep those medical receipts from the years you didn't make HSA reimbursement withdrawals. Those past medical receipts act as tickets to tax-free withdrawals from your HSA at any time, and that money can be used for whatever your heart desires.

If you're married, keep your spouse's medical receipts as well. Those receipts act as tickets to tax-free withdrawals from your HSA too, even if they never participated in your plan!

It doesn't matter if those medical receipts are from eight years ago or from last week. If you had a high-deductible health plan and HSA in the year of the medical expense, and you didn't reimburse your HSA for those expenses (no double-dipping), you can withdraw the equivalent amount from your HSA tax-free at any time.

I've broken down your options into three easy-to-follow strategies. The farther down the list, the more savings you'll generate, but even the Take the Money Now Strategy saves you big bucks:

Take the Money Now Strategy

This strategy saves you money today, not down the road. If you're looking to maximize your take-home pay for the year, use those tax-free dollars in your HSA to pay out-of-pocket medical expenses for you and your dependents as they occur during the plan year.

Many plans come with a debit card, making it easy to make tax-free withdrawals. Be sure to credit only HSA-deductible expenses.

Unlike the other strategies that delay some of the gratification, you get it all now. How much do you save versus using after-tax dollars to pay for your out-of-pocket medical expenses? It depends on your marginal tax bracket.

The HSA Double-Dip Strategy

Use the Double-Dip Strategy if you like the idea of using tax-free dollars now for you and your dependents' out-of-pocket medical expenses, while still saving and investing some money for the future.

Making a good estimate of your projected medical expenses for the year is the key to using this strategy successfully. Once again, good medical record-keeping from previous years helps you arrive at a more accurate estimate.

Assuming your estimate for medical expenses is below the HSA contribution limit for the year, inject that extra cash into your *customized investment plan* for your HSA.

Don't invest the money reserved for that year's medical expenses. Put those funds into an account where your principal is not at risk. Stick with the account attached to your debit card. A money market, savings account, or short-term bond fund option would also be appropriate.

Take it to the Max Strategy

Want to build your wealth over your working years faster than you ever thought possible? Your HSA, along with other tax-advantaged accounts like 401(k)-type plans and IRAs, can help you achieve your longer-term financial goals sooner rather than later.

Make the maximum HSA contribution each year. Do not reimburse yourself for any medical expenses. Pay for your out-of-pocket medical expenses with non-HSA money and invest those contributions for your financial future instead.

Good record keeping is especially important with this option. You not only want to save those unreimbursed medical receipts (they act as tickets to your tax-free cash) but also be on the safe side and save that year's tax return as well, even if it's from more than seven years ago.

Take it to the Max Example

If you started saving and investing the maximum contribution in your HSA in 2025, look at how much tax-free bank you could potentially accumulate by your projected retirement date.

The following example assumes an 8% compounded yearly return, the maximum yearly contribution, and a 3% yearly increase in future maximum contribution amounts.

Year	Contribution Amount (single)	Contribution Amount (family)	Year End (single)	Year End (family)
2025	$4,300	$8,550	$4,730	$9,405
2035	$5,740	$11,100	$98,700	$196,250
2045	$7,715	$15,340	$372,100	$740,000
2055	$12,400	$22,650	$1,124,650	$2,233,000
2065	$28,130	$41,900	$3,258,000	$6,340,000

Timing Your HSA Contribution

In line with this "take it to the max" strategy, if you fund your HSA yourself, try to make the entire contribution as early in the year as you can. If you do this year after year, over time, it can make a big positive difference.

If you're making contributions via your employer and payroll contributions, try to get as much money into your HSA as soon as possible (if given the option and you can afford it).

If you're making your own contribution, you have until April 15th in the year following the coverage year to make HSA contributions. (You have until April 15, 2027, to make a 2026 HSA contribution.) However, given those positive statistics, why wait?

Developing a Withdrawal Strategy

If you've decided to "take it to the max," make sure you add that extra $1,000 to your annual contribution amount starting with the year of your 55th birthday.

My example does not consider the $1,000 "catch-up" amount when you reach age 55, so your savings and earnings could be even more than depicted.

The More You Make the More You Save

Your marginal tax bracket is the last tax bracket you fall into when you pay your taxes. For 2026, everyone starts paying taxes at 10%. If your taxable income is high enough, you then progress to the 12% tax bracket, then 22, 24, 32, 35, and finally 37%, the highest of the seven brackets.

So, if you're in the 35% tax bracket, you save 35% versus paying with money after-tax. The higher your marginal tax bracket, the more you save.

Can I Really Earn Double-Digit Returns?

Did you balk a bit at my assumed 8% rate of return in my examples? If you did, I understand. That 8% per year rate of return is not realistic for those of us approaching or already in retirement (unless we experience runaway inflation again); However, if the stock market's history repeats, those of you with longer time horizons for investment—as depicted by the example—*can* attain an 8% per year average return or better.

Risk and the Take it to the Max Strategy

Don't think this strategy is just for the risk-takers among us. You can use this strategy even if you are a conservative investor.

If you're a super-conservative investor, you'll set up an investment plan for yourself that is more concerned with capital preservation than double-digit per year gains. And no, you won't realize those lofty yearly returns. Even if you are aggressive, but your time horizon is very short, the time for double-digit returns has passed.

More aggressive investors who believe the stock market's history will repeat itself will use a more aggressive allocation mix. If they're right, a double-digit per year return is possible.

However, if the stock market's stellar history does not repeat itself, now our more conservative investors could end up with more money.

We can't predict the stock market's future, but we can position our investment plan appropriately for our time horizon and risk tolerance.

HSA Withdrawals in Retirement

Ideally, you'll have multiple tax-advantaged accounts to tap in retirement, including your Health Savings Account. What tax-advantaged accounts you tap and when depends on your situation.

If you used the Take the Money Now strategy, unless you were lucky and super-healthy, most of your HSA is already spent. However, if you employed one of the latter two strategies (The HSA Double-Dip or Take It to the Max), things could get interesting. So, what are your options?

First and foremost, remember that if you still have unreimbursed medical expenses from the past, that money can be withdrawn at any time tax-free, no matter what your age or reason for the withdrawal. Of course, current medical expenses for you, your spouse, and any dependents are considered qualified withdrawals too.

Reaching Medicare Age

Once you're eligible for Medicare (currently age 65), you can no longer contribute to an HSA; However, Medicare premiums (for parts A, B, and D) are considered qualified medical expenses and an eligible HSA expense. (If you're under age 65, your insurance premiums are *not* considered a qualified medical expense.)

You can now make unqualified taxable withdrawals without that nasty 20% penalty if you wish, but tax will still be owed. Of course, if you wait to reimburse yourself for HSA-eligible expenses, the withdrawals are 100% tax-free.

It's a nice feeling to have some HSA funds leftover in retirement. Your healthcare costs at that age and up will more than likely be higher going forward, even with Medicare. Then there is the potential need for long-term care, which is *not* covered by Medicare.

What if You Get Hit by a Bus?

It would be a bummer if you never got a chance to spend your windfall. What happens to that money if you get hit by a bus (or some other unfortunate event happens that results in your untimely death)?

Luckily, your HSA comes with a beneficiary statement, just like your 401(k) or IRA. Properly filling out that form assures your money is passed along seamlessly and inexpensively to your loved ones without having to go through probate.

If you're married, your spouse is more than likely to inherit your HSA. That surviving spouse can use it just as you could have used it if you had looked both ways before crossing the street.

They can use any unreimbursed medical expenses for tax-free withdrawals, to pay for their out-of-pocket medical expenses and Medicare premiums, as well as make taxable withdrawals for non-medical reasons.

Your HSA will not pass tax-free to non-spouse beneficiaries. Non-spouse beneficiaries must pay tax on HSA monies in the year of your death, and the ability to use the money tax-free for healthcare expenses is lost.

That's still a good deal for your non-spouse beneficiary, but they could be stuck with a hefty tax bill in the year of the inheritance.

State Income Taxes and Your Withdrawals

So far, I've only talked about *federal* tax liability. Unfortunately, there are a few greedy states in the United States of America that sock you for state tax when you withdraw money from your HSA.

If you live in a state with no state income tax (currently Alaska, Florida, South Dakota, Tennessee, Texas, Nevada, Washington, and Wyoming), you obviously owe no state tax when you withdraw money from your HSA, but you can't deduct your contribution in the year you make it on your yearly state tax return like you can in most states that have a state tax.

States That Tax Your HSA Distributions

California and New Jersey sock you with state tax on your HSA withdrawals. I'm a California resident and have reluctantly paid state tax on my withdrawals from my HSA. Hopefully, the California legislature will change this rule and cut me and others some slack!

Websites for California and New Jersey
California:
https://www.ftb.ca.gov/index.shtml?disabled=true

New Jersey: *http://www.state.nj.us/treasury/taxation/*

New Hampshire doesn't get you with state tax on your HSA withdrawals, but they do tax the part of your HSA withdrawals attributable to dividends and interest.

Website for New Hampshire
New Hampshire:
https://www.nh.gov/residents/taxes.html

Like federal tax laws, state tax laws can be complex and subject to change. Be sure to have a qualified tax professional or up-to-date software for your state of residence to help you determine how much tax you'll owe (if any) on your HSA withdrawals come tax time.

This is why a lot of folks choose to move to another state (or country) when they retire. By moving, you can avoid not only state tax on your HSA withdrawals but also withdrawals from other accounts that are taxable, like your traditional IRA, 401(k), 403(b), 457, or other taxable retirement account.

Be Smarter with Your Money

Treating your Health Savings Account like a supercharged investment vehicle makes sense. So does investing in other tax-advantaged investment accounts. Although none possess all the advantages of an HSA, you'll still earn a higher after-tax rate of return than you would in regular taxable accounts (everything else being equal).

That means taking full advantage of employer-sponsored plans, including 401(k)s, 403(b)s, 457s, and the like. They offer the ability to save a lot more money in a tax-advantaged manner than an HSA.

Don't forget about any IRA opportunities. Making traditional IRA and/or Roth IRA contributions makes sense for a variety of reasons, even if you're offered a retirement plan at work.

I once again urge you to take full advantage of every tax break your Uncle Sam affords. Don't even think about investing elsewhere until you've maxed out these accounts.

For example, if you're investing in a regular taxable account and not fully utilizing all your tax-advantaged investment options, I urge you to reconsider that strategy.

Save Each and Every Paycheck

During your working years, no matter how old you are or what stage in life you're at, try to save at least 15% (to start) of what you make toward your financial goals. Supersavers and those with higher incomes can save a significantly higher percentage.

That's 15% of your gross paycheck every time you get paid. This is the easiest way to save money. Don't forget to include your payroll contributions to your employer's 401(k)-type plan in that 15%: Those monies are going toward your financial goal of a comfortable retirement.

Try to mimic how a 401(k)-type plan works as far as saving for other financial goals. For example, say you're saving for the down payment on a house and your kid's college education in addition to retirement.

As soon as you're paid, take the appropriate percentage of your paycheck, and inject those monies into the customized investment plans you created for each goal.

Assume your savings goal is 20% per paycheck. Split it up appropriately. For example, you could assign a 10% payroll deduction to your 401(k)-type plan and 5% each to the other two goals.

Juggling Multiple Goals
At times, you may choose to re-prioritize your goals. For instance, you may temporarily want to divert funds to one particular goal.

Perhaps you'd like to buy that house sooner rather than later? Reduce your retirement contributions to 5% (assuming you're offered a 5% employer match, and you don't want to miss out on that free cash) and divert the rest, plus all college fund cash, to the house goal.

Even though you will have to readjust your savings later to make up for any shortfalls, it's all good. Buying that house is probably going to be an excellent investment.

Favor Prosperity Goals
Be reasonable about saving for financial goals that detract from your net worth or depreciate, like an expensive vacation or a new car. Try to favor those prosperous, longer-term goals and become financially independent sooner.

All of us need to make decisions daily as to whether we are going to save for the future or spend our money and enjoy life now. Taking a percentage of the gross right off the top makes it easier to save.

Paying Yourself First

I call this strategy "pay-yourself-first." By taking the money right off the top (your savings percentage) and putting it where it's going to do the most good (your customized investment plans for your financial goals), it's the best way I know of building your wealth over your working years.

Track Your Expenses Accurately

It helps if you can improve your expense tracking, especially if you incorporate my pay yourself first strategy. Remember, lowering your savings rate to account for any overspending is no longer an option because your financial goals have already been funded.

Tracking your spending as accurately as possible will help. Assign expense categories for all the ways you spend money, along with monthly budget amounts for each. Update them halfway through the month. Pay particular attention to any problematic categories you've discovered.

Consider converting all your expense categories to "fixed expenses," even ones that are periodic or variable. Assigning a fixed monthly amount to all your periodic and variable expenses ensures you have the money to pay that periodic bill or a higher variable bill when it comes due.

As an example, say you pay property tax on your house twice a year. Add those two bills together and divide by twelve. Save a little property tax each month, even in the ten months the bill isn't due. (Depending on your percentage of home equity, your lender may already be collecting monthly property tax payments from you.)

Set that money aside or consider opening another free checking or savings account to hold those funds until you need them. This ensures you have the money to pay that bill when it comes due.

Even though setting up this type of monthly budget may take a little longer initially, it makes tracking your expenses infinitely easier going forward: Every month's budget is the same!

Additionally, you can spend your leftover money at the end of the month with a clear conscience, knowing you are truly under budget.

How Much Can You Save?

You don't have to settle for a 15% savings rate. That's what I deem as the bare minimum. Depending on your circumstances, age, and income level, you may be able to save a much higher percentage.

A 17%, 20%, 25%, or even a 30% plus savings rate is possible. When it comes right down to it, anything within reason—even anything out of reason if we want it bad enough—is within our grasp.

It's the investors who can save that extra one or two percent that will build their wealth over their working years faster. They'll be the ones who will realize even the loftiest of financial goals.

So, what's your savings percentage? If you're planning to track your savings and expenses accurately, that's half the battle. If you're not tracking your expenses, you're overspending, it's just human nature.

Striving to be thriftier and more frugal in those more discretionary expense categories is another way of increasing your savings percentage. So is having clearly defined financial goals. A clearly defined goal helps you realize that practically anything is financially possible and will help you save even more.

Let me leave you with one last savings strategy. The next time you get a raise, instead of spending that extra money, apply the raise to your savings percentage. Continuing that strategy in whole or part going forward is a great way to move your savings percentage higher.

Put your money where it is going to do the most good—toward your financial goals. Remember, these are goals that are going to have a profound effect on you and your loved ones.

Maximize your earnings by designing a customized investment plan for all your financial goals. Use tax-advantaged entities like Health Savings Accounts, employer-sponsored retirement plans, and IRAs whenever possible.

You've got better things to worry about than money. Once you get your financial house in order, you can concentrate on more important things like your passions, family, and friends.

###

About Keith Dorney

I'm glad you decided to invest in a Health Savings Account. As you now know, investing in one is a great way to save on medical expenses, reduce your tax liability, and build wealth.

Looking for more? There are other accounts you can invest in that also offer advantages, tax-related and otherwise. A couple of my favorites are employer Roth options and Roth IRAs.

If you enjoyed this book and are looking for more, check out *A Beginners Guide to Roth IRAs and 401(k) Type Plans*. If you have a Roth option at work or are interested in Roth IRAs, it's a must-read.

Want to attain financial independence sooner rather than later? Be sure to read all four books in my *Becoming Financially Independent* series. See more at https://keithdorney.com.

I was a licensed Certified Financial Planner® for 16 years and earned degrees from the University of San Francisco and Penn State. After moving on from the NFL, my wife Katherine and I settled in Sonoma County, California, where we raised our two kids and still reside.

When not teaching and writing, I enjoy hanging out in the garden and spending time with family and friends.

Detailed Table of Contents

Table of Contents 7
A Diamond Among Your Employee Benefits 9
   Get Ready for Open Enrollment 12
      Flexible Spending Account versus HSA 12
      Qualified Medical Expenses 13
   Want a Quadruple Tax Break? 13
      Tax Break #1 13
      Tax Break #2 14
      Tax Break #3 15
      Tax Break #4 16
   Unused Money Rolls Forward 16
      When You Reach Age 65 17
      Substitute for Long Term Care Insurance 18
      Best Case Scenario 18
   Not For Everyone 19
Choosing the Right Insurance Coverage 21
   Wellness Services 21
   Low-Deductible Health Plan 22
   High-Deductible Health Plan 23
      Minimum Deductible Limits 24

Out-of-Pocket Maximums 25
Understanding "Insurance Speak" 25
   Premium 25
   Deductible 26
   Coinsurance 26
   Insurance Tiers 26
Understanding Coverage Acronyms 27
   HMO (Health Maintenance Organization) 28
   EPO (Exclusive Provider Organization) 28
   PPO (Preferred Provider Organization) 28
   HDHP (High-Deductible Health Plan) 29
Choosing the Right Health Savings Account 31
   Minimize Your Investment Expenses 32
      Index Funds Versus Actively Managed Funds 33
      Exchange-Traded Funds 34
      Investing with Vanguard® 35
   Recommendations for HSA Custodian 35
      HSA Bank® 35
      Fidelity® 36
The Importance of Good Medical Record Keeping 37
   Maximizing Your Tax-free Earnings 38
   IRS Form 8889 39

IRS Form 1099-SA 40
HSA Eligible Medical Expenses 43
   Deductibility of Long-Term Care Insurance
   Premiums 45
HSA *Ineligible* Medical Expenses 47
Health Savings Account Contribution Limits 49
   HSA Contribution Limits 49
   HSA "Catch-Up" Contribution 49
   HSA Contributions and Working Spouses 50
Developing a Withdrawal Strategy 51
   Take the Money Now Strategy 52
   The HSA Double-Dip Strategy 53
   Take it to the Max Strategy 54
      Take it to the Max Example 54
      Timing Your HSA Contribution 55
      The More You Make the More You Save 56
      Can I Really Earn Double-Digit Returns? 56
      Risk and the Take it to the Max Strategy 57
   HSA Withdrawals in Retirement 58
      Reaching Medicare Age 58
      What if You Get Hit by a Bus? 59
State Income Taxes and Your Withdrawals 61

- States That Tax Your HSA Distributions 61
  - Websites for California and New Jersey 62
  - Website for New Hampshire 62
- Be Smarter with Your Money 63
  - Save Each and Every Paycheck 64
    - Juggling Multiple Goals 65
    - Favor Prosperity Goals 65
    - Paying Yourself First 66
  - Track Your Expenses Accurately 66
  - How Much Can You Save? 67
- About Keith Dorney 71
- Detailed Table of Contents 73

www.ingramcontent.com/pod-product-compliance
Lightning Source LLC
Chambersburg PA
CBHW060657030426
42337CB00017B/2660